She Persisted

....

CLAUDETTE COLVIN

—INSPIRED BY—

She Persisted

by Chelsea Clinton & Alexandra Boiger

CLAUDETTE COLVIN

Written by
Lesa Cline-Ransome

Interior illustrations by
Gillian Flint

PHILOMEL

PHILOMEL BOOKS
An imprint of Penguin Random House LLC, New York

Visit us online at penguinrandomhouse.com.

Library of Congress Cataloging-in-Publication Data is available.

Printed in the United States of America

HC ISBN 9780593115831
PB ISBN 9780593115848

10 9 8 7 6 5 4 3 2 1

Edited by Jill Santopolo.
Design by Ellice M. Lee.
Text set in LTC Kennerley.

For my girls:
Ava Robinson and Rihanna Perry
Young, bold and brave

She
Persisted

....

She Persisted: HARRIET TUBMAN

She Persisted: CLAUDETTE COLVIN

She Persisted: SALLY RIDE

She Persisted: VIRGINIA APGAR

She Persisted: NELLIE BLY

She Persisted: SONIA SOTOMAYOR

She Persisted: FLORENCE GRIFFITH JOYNER

She Persisted: RUBY BRIDGES

She Persisted: CLARA LEMLICH

She Persisted: MARGARET CHASE SMITH

She Persisted: MARIA TALLCHIEF

She Persisted: HELEN KELLER

She Persisted: OPRAH WINFREY

DEAR READER,

As Sally Ride and Marian Wright Edelman both powerfully
said, "You can't be what you can't see." When Sally Ride said
that, she meant that it was hard to dream of being an astronaut,
like she was, or a doctor or an athlete or anything at all if you
didn't see someone like you who already had lived that dream.
She especially was talking about seeing women in jobs that
historically were held by men.

I wrote the first *She Persisted* and the books that came
after it because I wanted young girls—and children of all
genders—to see women who worked hard to live their dreams.
And I wanted all of us to see examples of persistence in the face
of different challenges to help inspire us in our own lives.

I'm so thrilled now to partner with a sisterhood of
writers to bring longer, more in-depth versions of these stories
of women's persistence and achievement to readers. I hope
you enjoy these chapter books as much as I do and find them
inspiring and empowering.

And remember: If anyone ever tells you no, if anyone
ever says your voice isn't important or your dreams are too big,
remember these women. They persisted and so should you.

Warmly,

Chelsea Clinton

CLAUDETTE COLVIN

TABLE OF CONTENTS

....

·····································

Born Famous

O n September 5, 1939, before Claudette Colvin became Claudette Colvin, her family didn't know what they would call her. But once they saw her perfectly high cheekbones, they named her after Claudette Colbert, the famed high-cheekboned actress and well-loved beauty.

One Claudette was Black and one was white. One Claudette was from Birmingham, Alabama, and one lived in Hollywood, California. But only one Claudette's brave stand for civil rights would push her into the spotlight by the time she was fifteen years old. And that Claudette was Claudette Colvin.

One year after Claudette was born, her little sister, Delphine, arrived and they both were sent to live with their aunt Mary and uncle Q.P. Colvin in a small town called Pine Level, Alabama. Q.P. fixed up the bedroom left behind by their grown daughter, Velma, who was away teaching school. Both Mary and Q.P. were happy to have their home filled with little girls again.

Mary and Q.P. raised and loved Claudette and Delphine like daughters and the girls loved them back just the same. Before long they called them Mom and Dad. Together, they made a family.

Claudette was just as tiny as could be when

she arrived in Pine Level, but soon she grew as tall as a weed, and skinny as one too.

It was Q.P. who built their home, by himself from the ground up. Small and simple, it looked like many of the other sharecropper homes in Pine Level that sat on land rented from white landowners.

Sharecroppers like Mary and Q.P. were farmers who planted and grew their plots in exchange for a small share of the profit from the crops they harvested. Claudette's family didn't have much, but the house had everything Claudette needed. Best of all, there were chickens, cows, pigs, a horse she could ride and a dog named Bell.

Every second Sunday of the month, the Reverend H.H. Johnson traveled from Montgomery to Pine Level to preach the Sunday service on what folks called Big Meeting Sunday. From midday to well after dark, Claudette sat with her parents in the pews through regular service, selections from the choir and the glee club, Reverend Johnson's afternoon sermon, early supper, Reverend Johnson's evening sermon and a late supper. Then everyone headed home in the dark, their bellies filled with good food and their hearts filled with the good word.

Claudette loved church so much that she set up chairs in her backyard, sang hymns, read scrip-

ture and shouted out sermons with her best friend Annie Ruth Baines, pretending to be in church even when she wasn't.

Pine Level had just one general store, one church and a one-room white wooden schoolhouse. At Spring Hill School, the classes went from first to sixth grade with only one teacher giving all the lessons in the large room. In the middle was a pot-bellied stove to keep them warm on the days when the Alabama sun did not.

Seated two to a desk, Claudette and her class-mates learned their letters and numbers. But after first grade, when Claudette started reading the Bible and dictionary on her own, the teacher had to move her up to sit with the third graders.

Two things folks in Pine Level knew about little Claudette Colvin: she loved learning and God in equal measure.

······························

CHAPTER 2

Why Aren't Black People Treated as Equals?

Why don't the stars fall? When Bell dies, will she go to heaven? Claudette began and ended her day with questions. When her mom and dad didn't have the answers, or were just plain tired of the asking, Claudette turned to friends and neighbors.

Claudette knew that across an ocean and what seemed like a world away, the United States was fighting a war against Germany and a man named Adolf Hitler. At home, Claudette tried to under‑ stand a world where Black people were treated like enemies instead of allies. Like strangers instead of neighbors. She wondered why Black people weren't allowed to go to the same schools as white people, live in the same neighborhoods or even worship in the same churches when they all prayed to the same god.

In Sunday school, the Bible taught that God created everyone equal, but Claudette wondered, *Why aren't Black people treated as equals?* Reverend Johnson liked that Claudette asked questions, but even he didn't have the answers she needed.

When a relative passed away and willed a small rickety home, perched at the top of the King Hill section of Montgomery on 658 Dixie Drive, to Claudette's mom, she and her family packed up and moved out to make a new life in a new city.

In Montgomery, her mom took on work as a maid, her dad as a yard man, tending to the homes and gardens of Montgomery's wealthier white families. With her best friend Annie still back in Pine Level, Claudette and her little sister, Delphine, became even closer than before. In the bedroom they shared, the two knelt each night in prayer:

Our Father, who art in heaven,

Hallowed be thy name.

Thy kingdom come,

Thy will be done . . .

Then, side by side, they crawled into bed and under the covers. Claudette spelled out the new words she'd learned in school for her little sister. Delphine twisted and turned her arms and legs to show Claudette her dance moves. Sometimes they stayed up half the night, spelling, dancing, laughing and whispering.

The community of King Hill sat up above the rest of Montgomery, but because King Hill had unpaved streets and houses where you could see clear through to the back door from the front, the rest of Montgomery looked down on the residents of King Hill. But whatever people may have felt about King Hill, Claudette loved the nearby park and the neighbors who sat on their porches and looked out for each other like family, just like back in Pine Level.

In downtown Montgomery, Claudette was reminded that being Black in this city meant that she was a second-class citizen in the eyes of the white people. From the doctor's office to Kress's five-and-dime store on Monroe Street, Claudette saw that Montgomery was two different cities in one: one for white people and one for Black people. Black people weren't allowed to use the fitting rooms to try on clothing in shops. Black people who needed shoes weren't allowed to try them on at the store, so at home they had to trace the shape of their feet onto brown paper bags and match their size to the shoes they wanted.

And Black people weren't allowed to be seen by doctors until all the white patients had been seen first. At Oak Park, the nicest park in the city of Montgomery, Black people could only pass through without sitting on the benches or having a picnic or playing a ball game like the white families were allowed to do.

And when Claudette rode the city bus after school in downtown Montgomery, she and other Black people had to board the bus, drop their dime in the fare box next to the bus driver, then get off the bus and reenter through the back door so they did not walk past the rows of white people sitting in the whites-only section in front. If the white section filled with riders, the driver would yell to

the Black riders in back, "I need that seat!" and
the white riders could take some of the seats meant
for Black riders too.

Claudette obeyed her parents by minding her
manners and following the rules that had been in

place since long before she was born. This colorful city, where Claudette could get a good education and even earn the chance to go to college and study to become a lawyer, was also a city of Black and white.

CHAPTER 3

Why Delphine?

Always the youngest and smallest in her class, Claudette stood tall as one of the best in spelling bees. She won the weekly contests with the help of afternoon trips to the library and a dictionary bought by her parents. Claudette loved school, and after eighth grade ended and the long summer days grew shorter, Claudette looked forward to entering Booker T. Washington High School as a freshman.

But just two weeks before her first day of high school was set to begin, her sister Delphine awoke by her side with a fever. When Delphine's temperature climbed higher and higher all day, her parents knew that something more had to be done.

She was rushed to St. Jude Hospital, where they treated both Black and white patients equally.

Doctors knew instantly that Delphine had contracted the polio virus that was spreading through homes across the country that summer. Claudette begged to be by Delphine's side, but was kept away to stop the virus from infecting her, too.

As Delphine's temperature rose throughout another night, and her arms and legs that once twisted and turned in dance lay still by her sides, Claudette waited and prayed, prayed and waited. As the morning sun broke the next day, Delphine lost her battle to polio and died on September 5, 1952, Claudette's thirteenth birthday.

Claudette, the girl once filled with so many questions for God, now only had one: *Why Delphine?*

Claudette began her first day of high school lonely, grieving and missing her sister. Walking past the spot where Delphine had waited for her after school made the days long. Crawling into bed alone in the evenings made the nights longer. But Claudette knew Delphine would have wanted her to keep on keeping on.

Even though Booker T. Washington High School was in need of new textbooks and building repairs, the teachers who worked there built a strong foundation for their students with what little they had. In tenth grade, Claudette's history teacher Miss Lawrence taught them about African nations and Black history. When slavery and the Underground Railroad were discussed, Claudette dreamed of becoming like Harriet Tubman, who had escaped slavery and become an abolitionist, fighting to end slavery not just for people like her who had escaped, but for everyone, and hoped, like Harriet, to do something to uplift her people.

Claudette's favorite teacher was Miss Geraldine Nesbitt, a Montgomery native who had degrees in English from a college in Alabama and Columbia University in New York City. Miss Nesbitt, who taught English, brought in her own books from home to fill up their nearly empty class-room library. From poetry to Patrick Henry, the Bible to the Constitution, Miss Nesbitt's lessons taught Claudette and her classmates about history,

equality and justice. It was a class where they did as much talking as they did reading, and where Claudette could ask as many questions as she wanted.

In 1954, at the end of Claudette's sophomore year, the United States Supreme Court ruled that all schools were to be desegregated, and could no longer separate Black and white students, in the historic *Brown v. Board of Education* case. Brown stood for Oliver Brown, a Black man whose daughter wasn't allowed to go to the school closest to their house because of the color of her skin. Mr. Brown didn't think that was fair, and he brought the case to the Supreme Court. The Justices there all agreed with him, and their ruling meant that schools all across America would have to change.

Claudette and her classmates tried to imagine a world where they would be sharing a classroom with white students.

During Claudette's junior year, Booker T. Washington students spent the entire month of February discussing the injustice and inequality for Black people in Montgomery, and teachers and students studied some of the very same questions Claudette had been asking since she was a little girl.

Claudette realized the lessons she was learning were so much more important than spelling bees and math tests. After the loss of Delphine, Claudette began high school feeling she was powerless in fighting for her sister's life, but now she was learning there were plenty of other ways she could fight.

································

CHAPTER 4

Just Because I'm Black?

S pring began early in Alabama, and the warm
sunny afternoon of March 2, 1955, blanketed
the air with the scent of magnolia blossoms.

Claudette and her classmates made their way
from school to the Dexter Avenue and Bainbridge
Street bus stop to wait for the bus. With a dis-
count pink coupon slip, students could ride for half
price—a nickel, rather than the dime other passengers paid.

The green-and-gold city bus pulled up to their stop, and Claudette boarded the steps and handed her coupon and nickel to the driver. There were no white people on the Highland Gardens bus that afternoon, so the students were allowed to walk straight through to the seats for Black riders in the back rather than getting off the bus and reentering through the back door. Claudette took a seat midway down the aisle, next to the window, and piled her schoolbooks on her lap. Her classmates filled in the seats behind her, next to her and across the aisle.

As the bus made its way through downtown Montgomery, white riders began boarding at each stop and quickly filled the front seats. Claudette looked up to see a white woman standing at the row where she and her classmates were seated. In other cities with segregation laws, like Atlanta and

Nashville, there were also Black and white sec-tions, but Black people didn't have to give up their seats when the white sections were filled.

But Claudette only knew the rules in Mont-gomery. And she knew that if all the seats for white riders were filled, then the Black riders had to give up their seats for white passengers. But Claudette also knew what she had learned in Miss Nesbitt's class about her rights as a citizen. She had learned about people who took a stand for what they believed was right. Claudette wondered, *If I paid for a seat on the bus like every other passenger, why should I be forced to move just because I'm Black?*

She looked again at the white woman. She wasn't elderly like her mom, or expecting a baby like her neighbor Miss Hamilton, who had just boarded the bus and needed a seat to rest. When

her classmates in the seats across the aisle got up and moved to ones farther back, Claudette made her decision.

"Harriet Tubman's hands were pushing down on one shoulder and Sojourner Truth's hands were pushing down on the other shoulder . . . I couldn't move," Claudette later recalled.

"Why are you still sittin' there?" she heard the bus driver yell from his seat as he glared at her in his rearview mirror. "Get up, gal!" But Claudette stayed right where she was.

The bus kept moving, picking up more passengers, and then the driver stopped at the intersection of Bibb and Commerce streets and flagged down two white police officers. White passengers began screaming at Claudette to move. The officers got out of their police cruiser and came aboard the bus.

They spoke to the driver and quickly made their way toward the back and toward Claudette.

Claudette had never seen anyone refuse to give up their seat. Had never seen anyone talk back to a white police officer. As she watched the officers walking quickly back to her seat, she didn't know what would happen next, but she knew things would never be the same for her.

The bus stood idling as Black and white passengers sat silent, watching. When the officers reached her seat, one stood over Claudette and demanded, "Aren't you going to get up?"

Claudette gathered her courage and said through her tears, "It's my constitutional right to sit here as much as that lady. I paid my fare . . ."

Again they demanded Claudette get up, and again she told them, "No."

One of the officers grabbed her hands, the other grabbed her arm and they pulled her out of her seat and into the aisle. Her schoolbooks tumbled onto the floor. As they dragged her backward down the aisle and off the bus, one of the officers kicked her. But Claudette continued to scream, "It's my constitutional right!" all the way to the police cruiser. They shoved her into the back seat, cuffed her hands and shut the door. Crying, Claudette became more and more afraid as she listened to officers of the law call her every horrible word white people called Black people.

"Our father, who art in heaven,
Hallowed be thy name.
Thy kingdom come,
Thy will be done . . ."

Claudette began whispering the Lord's Prayer that she and Delphine used to recite by their bedside at night. And when she finished, she started in on the Twenty-Third Psalm to block out the officers' hateful words.

Even though Claudette was only fifteen years old, a minor, they drove her to the city jail instead of to the juvenile facility. Instead of letting her make a phone call home to her parents, they led her straight to a jail cell. When they closed the door and locked her in, Claudette knelt on the hard cement floor of her cell and prayed some more.

·····························

CHAPTER 5

What Happens Next?

While Claudette knelt in her jail cell, word of her arrest spread throughout the city of Montgomery. Her classmates from the bus called Claudette's mother at work, and her mother called Reverend Johnson, who went to the jail to pay Claudette's bail and bring her home.

"I think you just brought the revolution to Montgomery," Reverend Johnson told her proudly.

Neighbors lined the street waiting to greet

her when she arrived home, but Claudette was more focused on how angry her parents would be that she had disobeyed the law. But instead of being angry, her mother's only concern was that her daughter was out of jail. Everyone was happy to have Claudette home safe and in one piece, but her family knew that her arrest could bring trouble too. That night, as everyone went off to sleep, her father stayed awake, seated in his favorite chair in the front room with his shotgun across his lap, waiting for trouble from white people who might come to get revenge on Claudette and her family. Thankfully, it never came.

The next days didn't much feel like a revolution to Claudette. Back at school, her classmates at first wanted her to retell her story of what happened on the bus again and again, but soon they began to tease her with her own words. "It's my constitutional right," they laughed. Parents wondered if Claudette was a troublemaker and kept their children away from her. She was told to move north if she didn't like the way things worked in the South. Some teachers thought her arrest had made it harder on everyone else. But Miss Nesbitt wasn't one of them. She thought Claudette was brave. At church, Reverend Johnson led the entire congregation in prayer for the young woman who stood up to racism.

Claudette knew that with God and her family by her side, she couldn't go wrong with standing up for what was right. But she still needed a lawyer to defend her in court on the three charges of violating segregation laws, disturbing the peace and assaulting a police officer. Claudette would have to face a white judge and, depending on the verdict, possibly serve time in a reform school. For the first time ever, Claudette could see her dream of going off to college and becoming a lawyer slipping away as her mind wondered again and again, *What happens next?*

When E.D. Nixon, a Black leader in the community and part of the Montgomery chapter of the National Association for the Advancement of Colored People (NAACP), an organization that had been fighting for civil rights since 1909, got word that Claudette's family was in need of a lawyer, he knew just who to call. There were only two Black lawyers in Montgomery, and Fred Gray was one of them. At twenty-four years old, Fred Gray was barely older than Claudette, but he knew how to organize community leaders to help him get justice for his young client. He called on another young man, the energetic new pastor at Dexter Avenue Baptist Church named Dr. Martin Luther King Jr., and other Black leaders to meet with the police commissioner about Claudette's case. He warned Claudette and her parents how dangerous it could be for them. He needed to know if Claudette was sure she was ready to keep going.

"Yes, I am," she told him.

The NAACP youth group leader invited Claudette to come and speak to her group in the

hope that more young people would join the fight for civil rights. Claudette found a kind supporter in the woman, who introduced herself as Rosa Parks.

The community baked cookies and held fundraisers to help pay Claudette's attorney fees and she was lifted up in prayer. Fred Gray gathered witnesses to testify and coached Claudette on how to answer questions she would be asked. Black leaders came out to support Claudette, printing up flyers demanding justice and that all charges against her be dropped. The community was coming together like never before, and in the air, Black residents in Montgomery could feel that something was brewing. Something like a revolution.

....

CHAPTER 6

Who Wouldn't Cry?

When Claudette pulled up in front of the juvenile courthouse with her father on the morning of March 18, 1955, she was confident that by noon, her name would be cleared and soon she could go back to being a normal high school student. After all, her attorney was prepared, and he had entered a plea of not guilty. Gray was hoping to use Claudette's case and the words she shouted to the arresting officers to showcase how the city and the state of Alabama's segregation laws were unconstitutional and, according to the rules of the government, illegal. Fred Gray and Claudette Colvin were not only putting the segregated bus laws on trial, they were putting Jim Crow, the racist system of segregation in place since the end of slavery, on trial.

In the courtroom, community leaders Jo Ann Robinson and Reverend Ralph Abernathy sat behind Claudette and her attorney in the courtroom, while the student witnesses sat in the hall waiting to give their testimony. First, the arresting officers testified that Claudette had "fought" them by kicking and scratching. One falsely stated that Claudette had shouted that she was "just as good as white." In Montgomery, that type of statement from a Black person was a dangerous one to make. The prosecution even produced a letter from a white passenger who praised the officers as "gentlemen" in the calm and gentle way they treated Claudette before her arrest.

But the Black student witnesses offered completely different accounts of how Claudette was roughly handled and mistreated by the police officers on the bus. Gray himself called into question laws that discriminated against Montgomery's Black citizens. After Judge Hill heard from both the defense and the prosecution, he made his decision.

"Guilty!" he declared, slamming down his gavel before lunchtime even began.

Claudette was released into the custody of her parents and placed on probation indefinitely. She'd kept her feelings inside throughout the weeks of preparing for the trial, but now that she'd been branded a criminal with a record that would follow her like a shadow, the tears started and wouldn't stop. *Who wouldn't cry after hearing a guilty verdict?*

The next day residents of the capital city read the headline "Negro Girl Guilty of Violation of City Bus Segregation Law." The revolution that

had been brewing finally bubbled over. Many Black people no longer wanted to ride the buses, choosing instead to walk or carpool with those who had cars. Some wanted a complete boycott to protest Claudette's verdict. Others wondered if a teenager, a poor girl from King Hill, should even be the face of a boycott movement. And after the leaders poked and probed, met and argued, their verdict was no. But they did agree to appeal Claudette's conviction and ask the judge to reverse his decision. This time, Fred Gray managed to convince Judge Eugene Carter to drop two of Claudette's three charges, but Claudette still had to remain on probation and pay a fine.

After the trial, Claudette returned to the same high school in the same city, but not much else would ever be the same again for the residents of Montgomery. On December 1, 1955, just nine months after Claudette was found guilty of violating segregation laws, Rosa Parks, the NAACP youth coordinator who had befriended Claudette, also refused to give up her seat to a white passenger on a crowded city bus and was arrested. Rosa Parks's arrest kicked off a bus boycott lasting 381 days. Black residents walked and carpooled to school, work and church. To intimidate them and end the boycott, protestors were fired from jobs, received death threats, and were even bombed in their homes. Many were the victims of violence. But they vowed to keep walking until their demands for fairness were met.

Fred Gray sued the state of Alabama in the groundbreaking *Browder v. Gayle* case that challenged segregation laws, and Claudette Colvin, as one of the plaintiffs bringing the case to court, delivered a powerful account of what had happened. "The testimony of Miss Colvin and the others reinforced the constitution's position that you can't abridge the freedoms of the individual," cited one of the judges in the case.

Claudette's testimony, along with three others', ultimately led to the desegregation of Montgomery city buses. Before she testified, she bowed her head in prayer:

"Our Father, who art in heaven,
Hallowed be thy name . . ."

December 21, 1956, was the first day of integrated bus service in Montgomery, Alabama— Black people could now sit anywhere on the bus they wanted. And it all began with one brave girl who asked questions about fairness and justice and found her answer on a city bus in Montgomery, Alabama.

And that girl was Claudette Colvin.

HOW YOU CAN PERSIST

by Lesa Cline-Ransome

D o you have your own questions about justice
and equality like Claudette? Here are some
ways you can find answers:

1. Conduct research to learn how members
   in your family may have brought about
   change to their communities.

2. Read about others who are making
   a change in the world by using their

voices to stand up for what is right.

3. Know your rights. Visit your local library and ask for help in learning more about state and local laws.

4. Read a copy of the Constitution.

5. Talk to your friends and family about how they would like the world to change.

Acknowledgments

With each story I write, I am always transformed in some way by the subject and their story. Claudette was no exception. Her bravery in the face of hate and discrimination reminded me to stand up for what matters. Thank you to Claudette Colvin for this and so many other important lessons her story taught me. I am honored to have been entrusted with her story and especially thankful for those accompanied me on this journey: Editors extraordinaire Jill Santopolo and Talia Benamy, thank you for your attentiveness and assistance with research.

Chelsea Clinton for inviting me to be a part of the Persisterhood.

Thank you to my very honest and supportive readers James Ransome and Leila Ransome. One heck of an agent, Rosemary Stimola. The Cline family, friends Miriam Altshuler and Ann Burg.

And to the folks at the Rosa Parks Museum in Montgomery, Alabama, who bring history to life. And finally, to Phillip Hoose, whose stunning *Claudette Colvin: Twice Toward Justice*, guided me on way to Claudette's story.

∽ References ∾

Barnes, Brooks. "From Footnote to Fame in
Civil Rights History." *The New York Times.*
November 25, 2009.

Hoose, Phillip. *Claudette Colvin: Twice Toward
Justice.* New York: Melanie Kroupa Books,
2009.

Jacobson, Roni. "Claudette Colvin Explains Her
Role in the Civil Rights Movement." *Teen
Vogue.* October 19, 2017.

LESA CLINE-RANSOME is the author of many award-winning and critically acclaimed books for young readers, including *Not Playing By the Rules: 21 Female Athletes Who Changed Sports, Young Pele: Soccer's First Star, Before She Was Harriet, Overground Railroad, Finding Langston* and *Leaving Lymon*. She lives in the Hudson Valley region of New York with her family.

Photo credit: John Halpern

You can visit Lesa Cline-Ransome online at
lesaclineransome.com
or follow her on Twitter
@lclineransome

GILLIAN FLINT has worked as a professional illustrator since earning an animation and illustration degree in 2003. Her work has since been published in the UK, USA and Australia. In her spare time, Gillian enjoys reading, spending time with her family and puttering about in the garden on sunny days. She lives in the northwest of England.

You can visit Gillian Flint online at
gillianflint.com
or follow her on Twitter
@GillianFlint
and on Instagram
@gillianflint_illustration

CHELSEA CLINTON is the author of the #1 *New York Times* bestseller *She Persisted: 13 American Women Who Changed the World*; *She Persisted Around the World: 13 Women Who Changed History*; *She Persisted in Sports: American Olympians Who Changed the Game*; *Don't Let Them Disappear: 12 Endangered Species Across the Globe*; *It's Your World: Get Informed, Get Inspired & Get Going!*; *Start Now!: You Can Make a Difference*; with Hillary Clinton, *Grandma's Gardens* and *Gutsy Women*; and, with Devi Sridhar, *Governing Global Health: Who Runs the World and Why?* She is also the Vice Chair of the Clinton Foundation, where she works on many initiatives, including those that help empower the next generation of leaders. She lives in New York City with her husband, Marc, their children and their dog, Soren.

You can follow Chelsea Clinton on Twitter
@ChelseaClinton
or on Facebook at
facebook.com/chelseaclinton

ALEXANDRA BOIGER has illustrated nearly twenty picture books, including the She Persisted books by Chelsea Clinton; the popular Tallulah series by Marilyn Singer; and the Max and Marla books, which she also wrote. Originally from Munich, Germany, she now lives outside of San Francisco, California, with her husband, Andrea, daughter, Vanessa, and two cats, Luiso and Winter.

Photo credit: Vanessa Blasich

You can visit Alexandra Boiger online at
alexandraboiger.com
on follow her on Instagram
@alexandra_boiger

Don't miss the rest of the books in the

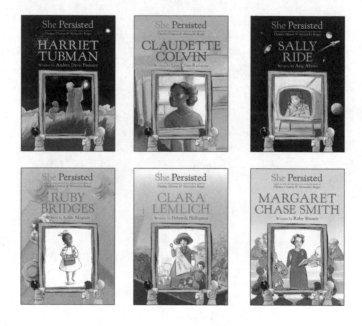

She Persisted series!

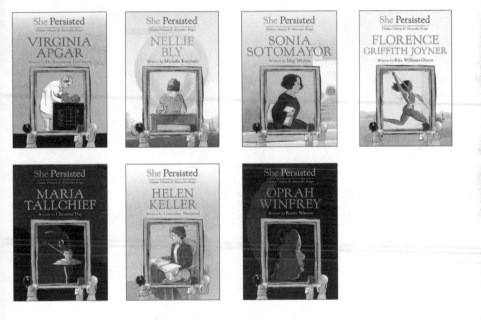